THE
Power
OF
THE HOLY
SPIRIT

THE *Power*
OF THE HOLY
SPIRIT

GEORGE
AND
HARRIET
GILLIES

Whitaker House

THE POWER OF THE HOLY SPIRIT

ISBN: 0-88368-511-6
Printed in the United States of America
Copyright © 1997 by Whitaker House

Whitaker House
30 Hunt Valley Circle
New Kensington, PA 15068

1 2 3 4 5 6 7 8 9 10 11 / 07 06 05 04 03 02 01 00 99 98 97

CONTENTS

ONE

Who and What Is
the Holy Spirit?

The Spirit of God.
"Therefore he who rejects this does not reject man, but God, who has also given us His Holy Spirit" (1 Thessalonians 4:8).

The Spirit of Jesus Christ, the Son of God.
"I will not leave you orphans; I will come to you" (John 14:18).
"And because you are sons, God has sent forth the Spirit of His Son into your hearts, crying out, 'Abba, Father!'" (Galatians 4:6).

The mind of Christ.
"Let this mind be in you which was also in Christ Jesus" (Philippians 2:5).

7

The Spirit of truth.

"The Spirit of truth, whom the world cannot receive, because it neither sees Him nor knows Him; but you know Him, for He dwells with you and will be in you" (John 14:17).

"But when the Helper comes, whom I shall send to you from the Father, the Spirit of truth who proceeds from the Father, He will testify of Me" (John 15:26).

The Comforter.

"And I will pray the Father, and he shall give you another Comforter, that he may abide with you for ever" (John 14:16 KJV).

"But the Comforter, which is the Holy Ghost, whom the Father will send in my name, he shall teach you all things, and bring all things to your remembrance, whatsoever I have said unto you" (John 14:26 KJV).

"But when the Comforter is come, whom I will send unto you from the Father, even the Spirit of truth, which proceedeth from the Father, he shall testify of me" (John 15:26 KJV).

"Nevertheless I tell you the truth; it is expedient for you that I go away: for if I go not away, the Comforter will not come unto you; but if I depart, I will send him unto you" (John 16:7 KJV).

The Spirit of the Father.

"For it is not you who speak, but the Spirit of your Father who speaks in you" (Matthew 10:20).

The Promise of the Father.

"Behold, I send the Promise of My Father upon you" (Luke 24:49).

"And being assembled together with them, He commanded them not to depart from Jerusalem, but to wait for the Promise of the Father" (Acts 1:4).

"That the blessing of Abraham might come upon the Gentiles in Christ Jesus, that we might receive the promise of the Spirit through faith" (Galatians 3:14).

Power.

"And He said to them, 'Assuredly, I say to you that there are some standing here who will not taste death till they see the kingdom of God present with power'" (Mark 9:1).

"But you shall receive power when the Holy Spirit has come upon you; and you shall be witnesses to Me in Jerusalem, and in all Judea and Samaria, and to the end of the earth" (Acts 1:8).

Power from on high.

"Behold, I send the Promise of My Father

9

upon you; but tarry in the city of Jerusalem until you are endued with power from on high" (Luke 24:49).

A gift of God, just as salvation is.

"Then Peter said to them, 'Repent, and let every one of you be baptized in the name of Jesus Christ for the remission of sins; and you shall receive the gift of the Holy Spirit'" (Acts 2:38).

"Peter said to him, 'Your money perish with you, because you thought that the gift of God could be purchased with money!'" (Acts 8:20).

"The love of God has been poured out in our hearts by the Holy Spirit who was given to us" (Romans 5:5).

"Therefore he who rejects this does not reject man, but God, who has also given us His Holy Spirit" (1 Thessalonians 4:8).

"If you then, being evil, know how to give good gifts to your children, how much more will your heavenly Father give the Holy Spirit to those who ask Him!" (Luke 11:13).

"God gave them the same gift as He gave us when we believed on the Lord Jesus Christ" (Acts 11:17).

"So God, who knows the heart, acknowledged them by giving them the Holy Spirit, just as He did to us" (Acts 15:8).

"This only I want to learn from you: Did you receive the Spirit by the works of the law, or by the hearing of faith?" (Galatians 3:2).

TWO

Where Is the Holy Spirit, and When Does He Appear?

Here, always.

"Lo, I am with you always, even to the end of the age" (Matthew 28:20).

"And I will pray the Father, and He will give you another Helper, that He may abide with you forever" (John 14:16).

"If you then, being evil, know how to give good gifts to your children, how much more will your heavenly Father give the Holy Spirit to those who ask Him!" (Luke 11:13).

He was with certain people prior to Pentecost, but not in them.

"But this He spoke concerning the Spirit, whom those believing in Him would receive; for

the Holy Spirit was not yet given, because Jesus was not yet glorified" (John 7:39).

"The Spirit of truth, whom the world cannot receive, because it neither sees Him nor knows Him; but you know Him, for He dwells with you and will be in you. I will not leave you orphans; I will come to you" (John 14:17–18).

Made available to all believers at Pentecost.

"Then Peter said to them, 'Repent, and let every one of you be baptized in the name of Jesus Christ for the remission of sins; and you shall receive the gift of the Holy Spirit'" (Acts 2:38).

Now.

"And it shall come to pass afterward that I will pour out My Spirit on all flesh; your sons and your daughters shall prophesy, your old men shall dream dreams, your young men shall see visions. And also on My menservants and on My maidservants I will pour out My Spirit in those days" (Joel 2:28–29).

"For a thousand years in Your sight are like yesterday when it is past, and like a watch in the night" (Psalms 90:4).

"Beloved, do not forget this one thing, that with the Lord one day is as a thousand years, and a thousand years as one day" (2 Peter 3:8).

"Jesus Christ is the same yesterday, today, and forever" (Hebrews 13:8).

"For the promise is to you and to your children, and to all who are afar off, as many as the Lord our God will call" (Acts 2:39).

"If you then, being evil, know how to give good gifts to your children, how much more will your heavenly Father give the Holy Spirit to those who ask Him!" (Luke 11:13).

Available now to Gentiles.

"That the Gentiles should be fellow heirs, of the same body, and partakers of His promise in Christ through the gospel" (Ephesians 3:6).

THREE

Why Be Saved and Baptized in the Holy Spirit?

To become a child of God.

"But as many as received Him, to them He gave the right to become children of God, to those who believe in His name: who were born, not of blood, nor of the will of the flesh, nor of the will of man, but of God" (John 1:12–13).

"For as many as are led by the Spirit of God, these are sons of God. For you did not receive the spirit of bondage again to fear, but you received the Spirit of adoption by whom we cry out, 'Abba, Father.' The Spirit Himself bears witness with our spirit that we are children of God, and if children, then heirs; heirs of God and joint heirs with Christ, if indeed we suffer

with Him, that we may also be glorified together. For I consider that the sufferings of this present time are not worthy to be compared with the glory which shall be revealed in us. For the earnest expectation of the creation eagerly waits for the revealing of the sons of God. For the creation was subjected to futility, not willingly, but because of Him who subjected it in hope; because the creation itself also will be delivered from the bondage of corruption into the glorious liberty of the children of God" (Romans 8:14–21).

"Therefore know that only those who are of faith are sons of Abraham. And the Scripture, foreseeing that God would justify the Gentiles by faith, preached the gospel to Abraham beforehand, saying, 'In you all the nations shall be blessed.' So then those who are of faith are blessed with believing Abraham" (Galatians 3:7–9).

"That the blessing of Abraham might come upon the Gentiles in Christ Jesus, that we might receive the promise of the Spirit through faith" (Galatians 3:14).

"And if you are Christ's, then you are Abraham's seed, and heirs according to the promise" (Galatians 3:29).

"And because you are sons, God has sent forth the Spirit of His Son into your hearts, *crying out, 'Abba, Father!' Therefore you are no longer a slave but a son, and if a son, then an heir of God through Christ"* (Galatians 4:6–7).

"Behold what manner of love the Father has bestowed on us, that we should be called children of God! Therefore the world does not know us, because it did not know Him. Beloved, now we are children of God; and it has not yet been revealed what we shall be, but we know that when He is revealed, we shall be like Him, for we shall see Him as He is" (1 John 3:1–2).

To be of Christ.

"But you are not in the flesh but in the Spirit, if indeed the Spirit of God dwells in you. Now if anyone does not have the Spirit of Christ, he is not His" (Romans 8:9).

"I have been crucified with Christ; it is no longer I who live, but Christ lives in me; and the life which I now live in the flesh I live by faith in the Son of God, who loved me and gave Himself for me" (Galatians 2:20).

"For as many of you as were baptized into Christ have put on Christ" (Galatians 3:27).

To become alive.

"It is the Spirit who gives life; the flesh profits nothing. The words that I speak to you are spirit, and they are life" (John 6:63).

"But if the Spirit of Him who raised Jesus from the dead dwells in you, He who raised Christ from the dead will also give life to your mortal bodies through His Spirit who dwells in you" (Romans 8:11).

To have life and peace.

"For to be carnally minded is death, but to be spiritually minded is life and peace" (Romans 8:6).

"I have been crucified with Christ; it is no longer I who live, but Christ lives in me; and the life which I now live in the flesh I live by faith in the Son of God, who loved me and gave Himself for me" (Galatians 2:20).

"For he who sows to his flesh will of the flesh reap corruption, but he who sows to the Spirit will of the Spirit reap everlasting life" (Galatians 6:8).

To have no condemnation.

"There is therefore now no condemnation to those who are in Christ Jesus, who do not walk according to the flesh, but according to the Spirit" (Romans 8:1).

To be free from the law of sin and death.

"For the law of the Spirit of life in Christ Jesus has made me free from the law of sin and

death. For what the law could not do in that it was weak through the flesh, God did by sending His own Son in the likeness of sinful flesh, on account of sin: He condemned sin in the flesh, that the righteous requirement of the law might be fulfilled in us who do not walk according to the flesh but according to the Spirit. For those who live according to the flesh set their minds on the things of the flesh, but those who live according to the Spirit, the things of the Spirit. For to be carnally minded is death, but to be spiritually minded is life and peace" (Romans 8:2–6).

"But you are not in the flesh but in the Spirit, if indeed the Spirit of God dwells in you....And if Christ is in you, the body is dead because of sin, but the Spirit is life because of righteousness" (Romans 8:9–10).

"For if you live according to the flesh you will die; but if by the Spirit you put to death the deeds of the body, you will live" (Romans 8:13).

"For I through the law died to the law that I might live to God" (Galatians 2:19).

"I say then: Walk in the Spirit, and you shall not fulfill the lust of the flesh. For the flesh lusts against the Spirit, and the Spirit against the flesh; and these are contrary to one another, so that you do not do the things that you wish. But if you are led by the Spirit, you

are not under the law" (Galatians 5:16–18).

So that *"the righteous requirement of the law might be fulfilled in us"* (Romans 8:4).

To be taught all things and to understand what Jesus said.

"The words that I speak to you are spirit, and they are life" (John 6:63).

"But the Helper, the Holy Spirit, whom the Father will send in My name, He will teach you all things, and bring to your remembrance all things that I said to you" (John 14:26).

"For our gospel did not come to you in word only, but also in power, and in the Holy Spirit and in much assurance" (1 Thessalonians 1:5).

"But you have an anointing from the Holy One, and you know all things" (1 John 2:20).

"But the anointing which you have received from Him abides in you, and you do not need that anyone teach you; but as the same anointing teaches you concerning all things, and is true, and is not a lie, and just as it has taught you, you will abide in Him" (1 John 2:27).

To have the testimony of Jesus.

"But when the Helper comes, whom I shall send to you from the Father, the Spirit of truth

who proceeds from the Father, He will testify of Me" (John 15:26).

To be effective witnesses unto Jesus.

"But you shall receive power when the Holy Spirit has come upon you; and you shall be witnesses to Me in Jerusalem, and in all Judea and Samaria, and to the end of the earth" (Acts 1:8).

"So Jesus said to them again, 'Peace to you! As the Father has sent Me, I also send you'" (John 20:21).

To be able to worship the Father in spirit and in truth.

"But the hour is coming, and now is, when the true worshipers will worship the Father in spirit and truth; for the Father is seeking such to worship Him. God is Spirit, and those who worship Him must worship in spirit and truth" (John 4:23–24).

To have Jesus glorified.

"He will glorify Me, for He will take of what is Mine and declare it to you" (John 16:14).

"For I consider that the sufferings of this present time are not worthy to be compared with the glory which shall be revealed in us" (Romans 8:18).

To receive the Promise of the Father.

"Behold, I send the Promise of My Father upon you; but tarry in the city of Jerusalem until you are endued with power from on high" (Luke 24:49).

"And being assembled together with them, He commanded them not to depart from Jerusalem, but to wait for the Promise of the Father" (Acts 1:4).

"That we might receive the promise of the Spirit through faith" (Galatians 3:14).

To know the joy that Jesus promised.

"He who has the bride is the bridegroom; but the friend of the bridegroom, who stands and hears him, rejoices greatly because of the bridegroom's voice. Therefore this joy of mine is fulfilled" (John 3:29).

"These things I have spoken to you, that My joy may remain in you, and that your joy may be full" (John 15:11).

"Most assuredly, I say to you that you will weep and lament, but the world will rejoice; and you will be sorrowful, but your sorrow will be turned into joy. A woman, when she is in labor, has sorrow because her hour has come; but as soon as she has given birth to the child, she no longer remembers the anguish, for joy that a human being has been born into the

world. Therefore you now have sorrow; but I will see you again and your heart will rejoice, and your joy no one will take from you. And in that day you will ask Me nothing. Most assuredly, I say to you, whatever you ask the Father in My name He will give you. Until now you have asked nothing in My name. Ask, and you will receive, that your joy may be full" (John 16:20–24).

To follow Christ's example.

"When He had been baptized, Jesus came up immediately from the water; and behold, the heavens were opened to Him, and He saw the Spirit of God descending like a dove and alighting upon Him" (Matthew 3:16).

"And immediately, coming up from the water, He saw the heavens parting and the Spirit descending upon Him like a dove" (Mark 1:10).

"When all the people were baptized, it came to pass that Jesus also was baptized; and while He prayed, the heaven was opened. And the Holy Spirit descended in bodily form like a dove upon Him, and a voice came from heaven which said, 'You are My beloved Son; in You I am well pleased'" (Luke 3:21–22).

"And John bore witness, saying, 'I saw the Spirit descending from heaven like a dove, and He remained upon Him'" (John 1:32).

To have a full and effective ministry.

"The Spirit of the LORD is upon Me, because He has anointed Me to preach the gospel to the poor; He has sent Me to heal the brokenhearted, to proclaim liberty to the captives and recovery of sight to the blind, to set at liberty those who are oppressed; to proclaim the acceptable year of the LORD" (Luke 4:18–19).

"The Spirit of the Lord GOD is upon Me, because the LORD has anointed Me to preach good tidings to the poor; He has sent Me to heal the brokenhearted, to proclaim liberty to the captives, and the opening of the prison to those who are bound; to proclaim the acceptable year of the LORD, and the day of vengeance of our God; to comfort all who mourn, to console those who mourn in Zion, to give them beauty for ashes, the oil of joy for mourning, the garment of praise for the spirit of heaviness; that they may be called trees of righteousness, the planting of the LORD, that He may be glorified" (Isaiah 61:1–3).

To boldly proclaim the Gospel.

"Praying always with all prayer and supplication in the Spirit, being watchful to this end with all perseverance and supplication for all the saints; and for me, that utterance may be given to me, that I may open my mouth boldly

26

to make known the mystery of the gospel, for which I am an ambassador in chains; that in it I may speak boldly, as I ought to speak" (Ephesians 6:18–20).

To receive the kingdom of God with power.

"And He said to them, 'Assuredly, I say to you that there are some standing here who will not taste death till they see the kingdom of God present with power'" (Mark 9:1).

"For the kingdom of God is not eating and drinking, but righteousness and peace and joy in the Holy Spirit" (Romans 14:17).

"It is no longer I who live, but Christ lives in me; and the life which I now live in the flesh I live by faith in the Son of God, who loved me and gave Himself for me" (Galatians 2:20).

To receive power from on high.

"But you shall receive power when the Holy Spirit has come upon you; and you shall be witnesses to Me in Jerusalem, and in all Judea and Samaria, and to the end of the earth" (Acts 1:8).

To be able not only to see, but also to enter into the kingdom of God.

"Jesus answered and said to him, 'Most assuredly, I say to you, unless one is born *again, he cannot see the kingdom of God.' Ni-codemus said to Him, 'How can a man be born when he is old? Can he enter a second time into his mother's womb and be born?' Jesus an-swered, 'Most assuredly, I say to you, unless one is born of water and the Spirit, he cannot enter the kingdom of God'"* (John 3:3–5).

To be partakers of the divine nature.

"By which have been given to us exceed-ingly great and precious promises, that through these you may be partakers of the divine nature, having escaped the corruption that is in the world through lust" (2 Peter 1:4).

"For I am persuaded that neither death nor life, nor angels nor principalities nor pow-ers, nor things present nor things to come, nor height nor depth, nor any other created thing, shall be able to separate us from the love of God which is in Christ Jesus our Lord" (Romans 8:38–39).

"But indeed for this purpose I have raised you up, that I may show My power in you, and that My name may be declared in all the earth" (Exodus 9:16).

To be shown things to come, things of Jesus, and things of the Father.

"However, when He, the Spirit of truth,

has come, He will guide you into all truth; for He will not speak on His own authority, but whatever He hears He will speak; and He will tell you things to come. He will glorify Me, for He will take of what is Mine and declare it to you. All things that the Father has are Mine. Therefore I said that He will take of Mine and declare it to you" (John 16:13–15).

To have the perfect prayer made when we do not know what to pray for.

"Likewise the Spirit also helps in our weaknesses. For we do not know what we should pray for as we ought, but the Spirit Himself makes intercession for us" (Romans 8:26).

To have intercession made for us.

"But the Spirit Himself makes intercession for us with groanings which cannot be uttered. Now He who searches the hearts knows what the mind of the Spirit is, because He makes intercession for the saints according to the will of God" (Romans 8:26–27).

The redemption of our bodies.

"Not only that, but we also who have the firstfruits of the Spirit, even we ourselves groan within ourselves, eagerly waiting for the adoption, the redemption of our body" (Romans 8:23).

29

To help our weaknesses.

"Likewise the Spirit also helps in our weaknesses" (Romans 8:26).

To follow the leading of the Spirit.

"For those who live according to the flesh set their minds on the things of the flesh, but those who live according to the Spirit, the things of the Spirit" (Romans 8:5).

"If we live in the Spirit, let us also walk in the Spirit" (Galatians 5:25).

To be guided into all truth.

"However, when He, the Spirit of truth, has come, He will guide you into all truth" (John 16:13).

"But you have an anointing from the Holy One, and you know all things" (1 John 2:20).

"The anointing which you have received from Him abides in you, and you do not need that anyone teach you; but as the same anointing teaches you concerning all things, and is true, and is not a lie, and just as it has taught you, you will abide in Him" (1 John 2:27).

To have righteousness, peace, and joy in the Spirit.

"For the kingdom of God is not eating and drinking, but righteousness and peace and joy

in the Holy Spirit" (Romans 14:17).

To be called according to God's purpose.
    *"And we know that all things work to-
gether for good to those who love God, to those
who are the called according to His purpose"*
(Romans 8:28).

To have the Spirit *"of power and of love and of
a sound mind"* (2 Timothy 1:7).

**To know that we are really baptized into one
body, which is Christ's church.**
    *"I will give you a new heart and put a new
spirit within you; I will take the heart of stone
out of your flesh and give you a heart of flesh. I
will put My Spirit within you and cause you to
walk in My statutes, and you will keep My
judgments and do them"* (Ezekiel 36:26–27).
    *"For by one Spirit we were all baptized into
one body; whether Jews or Greeks, whether
slaves or free; and have all been made to drink
into one Spirit"* (1 Corinthians 12:13).
    *"For you are all sons of God through faith
in Christ Jesus. For as many of you as were
baptized into Christ have put on Christ. There
is neither Jew nor Greek, there is neither slave
nor free, there is neither male nor female; for
you are all one in Christ Jesus. And if you are*

Christ's, then you are Abraham's seed, and heirs according to the promise" (Galatians 3:26–29).

"In Him you also trusted, after you heard the word of truth, the gospel of your salvation; in whom also, having believed, you were sealed with the Holy Spirit of promise" (Ephesians 1:13).

To have the fruit of the Spirit.

"But the fruit of the Spirit is love, joy, peace, longsuffering, kindness, goodness, faithfulness, gentleness, self-control. Against such there is no law" (Galatians 5:22–23).

"For the fruit of the Spirit is in all goodness, righteousness, and truth" (Ephesians 5:9).

FOUR

Who Can Receive the Baptism in the Holy Spirit?

One who is a born-again believer.

"For He whom God has sent speaks the words of God, for God does not give the Spirit by measure" (John 3:34).

"Assuredly, I say to you, unless you are converted and become as little children, you will by no means enter the kingdom of heaven" (Matthew 18:3).

"Then Peter said to them, 'Repent, and let every one of you be baptized in the name of Jesus Christ for the remission of sins; and you shall receive the gift of the Holy Spirit. For the promise is to you and to your children, and to all who are afar off, as many as the Lord our

God will call'" (Acts 2:38–39).

"But when they believed Philip as he preached the things concerning the kingdom of God and the name of Jesus Christ, both men and women were baptized. Then Simon himself also believed; and when he was baptized he continued with Philip, and was amazed, seeing the miracles and signs which were done. Now when the apostles who were at Jerusalem heard that Samaria had received the word of God, they sent Peter and John to them, who, when they had come down, prayed for them that they might receive the Holy Spirit. For as yet He had fallen upon none of them. They had only been baptized in the name of the Lord Jesus. Then they laid hands on them, and they received the Holy Spirit" (Acts 8:12–17).

One who is completely surrendered to God, obeying the Great Commandment.

"Then one of them, a lawyer, asked Him a question, testing Him, and saying, 'Teacher, which is the great commandment in the law?' Jesus said to him, '"You shall love the LORD your God with all your heart, with all your soul, and with all your mind." This is the first and great commandment"' (Matthew 22:35–38).

One who is a child of God.

"But as many as received Him, to them He gave the right to become children of God, to those who believe in His name" (John 1:12).

One who receives the kingdom of God as a child.

"Assuredly, I say to you, whoever does not receive the kingdom of God as a little child will by no means enter it" (Mark 10:15).

One who is willing to become a fool for Christ.

"Let no one deceive himself. If anyone among you seems to be wise in this age, let him become a fool that he may become wise" (1 Corinthians 3:18).

Anyone who meets the above conditions, whether he is a Jew or a Gentile.

"That the Gentiles should be fellow heirs, of the same body, and partakers of His promise in Christ through the gospel" (Ephesians 3:6).

FIVE

Who Is the Baptizer in the Holy Spirit?

Jesus is the Baptizer.

"He who is coming after me is mightier than I, whose sandals I am not worthy to carry. He will baptize you with the Holy Spirit and fire" (Matthew 3:11).

"And he preached, saying, 'There comes One after me who is mightier than I, whose sandal strap I am not worthy to stoop down and loose. I indeed baptized you with water, but He will baptize you with the Holy Spirit'" (Mark 1:7–8).

"John answered, saying to all, 'I indeed baptize you with water; but One mightier than I is coming, whose sandal strap I am not worthy

to loose. He will baptize you with the Holy
Spirit and fire'" (Luke 3:16).

"I did not know Him, but He who sent me
to baptize with water said to me, 'Upon whom
you see the Spirit descending, and remaining
on Him, this is He who baptizes with the Holy
Spirit'" (John 1:33).

**Jesus has the power to baptize in the Holy
Spirit.**

"And Jesus came and spoke to them, saying, 'All authority has been given to Me in
heaven and on earth'" (Matthew 28:18).

SIX

How Do You Know for Sure That You Have Received the Baptism in the Holy Spirit?

The Spirit can dwell with people and yet not be in them.

"The Spirit of truth, whom the world cannot receive, because it neither sees Him nor knows Him; but you know Him, for He dwells with you and will be in you" (John 14:17).

After conversion, one is not necessarily baptized in the Holy Spirit. See the example in Samaria.

"Now when the apostles who were at Jerusalem heard that Samaria had received the

word of God, they sent Peter and John to them, who, when they had come down, prayed for them that they might receive the Holy Spirit. For as yet He had fallen upon none of them" (Acts 8:14–16).

How did Peter and John know that the people had not received the baptism in the Holy Spirit?

"They had only been baptized in the name of the Lord Jesus" (Acts 8:16).

And then, how did Peter, John, and Simon the sorcerer know that the people had received the baptism after Peter and John had laid hands on them?

"Then they laid hands on them, and they received the Holy Spirit" (Acts 8:17).

Another example is the baptism at the house of Cornelius, a Gentile.

"There was a certain man in Caesarea called Cornelius, a centurion of what was called the Italian Regiment, a devout man and one who feared God with all his household, who gave alms generously to the people, and prayed to God always....So Cornelius said, 'Four days ago I was fasting until this hour; and at the ninth hour I prayed in my house, and behold, a man stood before me in bright

clothing, and said, "Cornelius, your prayer has been heard, and your alms are remembered in the sight of God. Send therefore to Joppa and call Simon here, whose surname is Peter. He is lodging in the house of Simon, a tanner, by the sea. When he comes, he will speak to you." So I sent to you immediately, and you have done well to come. Now therefore, we are all present before God, to hear all the things commanded you by God.' Then Peter opened his mouth and...while Peter was still speaking these words, the Holy Spirit fell upon all those who heard the word. And those of the circumcision who believed were astonished, as many as came with Peter, because the gift of the Holy Spirit had been poured out on the Gentiles also" (Acts 10:1–2, 30–34, 44–45).

How did the Jews know that the Gentiles had received the baptism?

"For they heard them speak with tongues and magnify God" (Acts 10:46).

The apostolic Jews in Jerusalem were very much upset, and so they contended with Peter for having gone to the Gentiles. They also could not believe that the Gentiles had been baptized in the Holy Spirit.

"Now the apostles and brethren who were

in Judea heard that the Gentiles had also received the word of God. And when Peter came up to Jerusalem, those of the circumcision contended with him, saying, 'You went in to uncircumcised men and ate with them!'" (Acts 11:1–3).

Peter explained it to them.

"And as I began to speak, the Holy Spirit fell upon them, as upon us at the beginning" (Acts 11:15).

The beginning was at Pentecost.

"And they were all filled with the Holy Spirit and began to speak with other tongues, as the Spirit gave them utterance" (Acts 2:4).

"When they heard these things they became silent; and they glorified God, saying, 'Then God has also granted to the Gentiles repentance to life'" (Acts 11:18).

The baptism at Ephesus at the hands of Paul.

"Paul, having passed through the upper regions, came to Ephesus. And finding some disciples he said to them, 'Did you receive the Holy Spirit when you believed?' So they said to him, 'We have not so much as heard whether there is a Holy Spirit.' And he said to them, 'Into what then were you baptized?' So they

said, 'Into John's baptism.' Then Paul said, 'John indeed baptized with a baptism of repentance, saying to the people that they should believe on Him who would come after him, that is, on Christ Jesus.' When they heard this, they were baptized in the name of the Lord Jesus. And when Paul had laid hands on them, the Holy Spirit came upon them, and they spoke with tongues and prophesied" (Acts 19:1–6).

The evidence was praying in an unknown tongue.

"And they were all filled with the Holy Spirit and began to speak with other tongues, as the Spirit gave them utterance" (Acts 2:4).

"For they heard them speak with tongues and magnify God" (Acts 10:46).

"And when Paul had laid hands on them, the Holy Spirit came upon them, and they spoke with tongues and prophesied" (Acts 19:6).

"And these signs will follow those who believe: In My name they will cast out demons; they will speak with new tongues" (Mark 16:17).

"The wind blows where it wishes, and you hear the sound of it, but cannot tell where it comes from and where it goes. So is everyone who is born of the Spirit" (John 3:8).

"Therefore tongues are for a sign, not to

those who believe but to unbelievers" (1 Corinthians 14:22).

Jesus said everyone born of the Spirit would hear the sound thereof.

"The wind blows where it wishes, and you hear the sound of it, but cannot tell where it comes from and where it goes. So is everyone who is born of the Spirit" (John 3:8).

You are no holier after receiving the baptism than you were before. But you now potentially have the power of Jesus within you to overcome evil and to be a witness for Christ. The Lord God lets it be your choice, your free will, as to how you use this wonderful Gift of God, or whether you bury this talent (Matthew 25:14–30) in the earth.

"But you shall receive power when the Holy Spirit has come upon you" (Acts 1:8).

SEVEN

What Are the Manifestations of the Holy Spirit?

The manifestations of the Holy Spirit are given for the profit of the church.

"But the manifestation of the Spirit is given to each one for the profit of all" (1 Corinthians 12:7).

1. The word of wisdom.

"For to one is given the word of wisdom through the Spirit" (1 Corinthians 12:8).

2. The word of knowledge.

"To another the word of knowledge

through the same Spirit" (1 Corinthians 12:8).

3. Faith.
"To another faith by the same Spirit" (1 Corinthians 12:9).

4. Gifts of healing.
"To another gifts of healings by the same Spirit" (1 Corinthians 12:9).

5. The working of miracles.
"To another the working of miracles" (1 Corinthians 12:10).

6. Prophecy.
"To another prophecy" (1 Corinthians 12:10).

7. Discerning of spirits.
"To another discerning of spirits" (1 Corinthians 12:10).

8. Different kinds of tongues.
"To another different kinds of tongues" (1 Corinthians 12:10).

9. Interpretation of tongues.
"To another the interpretation of tongues" (1 Corinthians 12:10).

These manifestations of the Holy Spirit should be administered in the *"more excellent way"* (1 Corinthians 12:31), which is with love.

"Though I speak with the tongues of men and of angels, but have not love, I have become sounding brass or a clanging cymbal. And though I have the gift of prophecy, and understand all mysteries and all knowledge, and though I have all faith, so that I could remove mountains, but have not love, I am nothing. And though I bestow all my goods to feed the poor, and though I give my body to be burned, but have not love, it profits me nothing" (1 Corinthians 13:1–3).

"Pursue love, and desire spiritual gifts" (1 Corinthians 14:1).

When you receive the baptism in the Holy Spirit, you get the potential to exercise all of the above nine manifestations. They are all in you. But you only use them one at a time as the Spirit leads you to do, for the Spirit divides all nine *"to each one individually as He wills"* (1 Corinthians 12:11).

EIGHT

Manifestation of Prophecy Desired in the Church

You should desire to prophesy.

"Desire spiritual gifts, but especially that you may prophesy" (1 Corinthians 14:1).

"Therefore, brethren, desire earnestly to prophesy, and do not forbid to speak with tongues" (1 Corinthians 14:39).

The purpose of prophecy is for *"edification and exhortation and comfort"* (1 Corinthians 14:3).

Prophecy edifies the church.

"He who speaks in a tongue edifies himself, but he who prophesies edifies the church" (1

Corinthians 14:4).

"For you can all prophesy one by one, that all may learn and all may be encouraged" (1 Corinthians 14:31).

Prophecy is greater in the church than even tongues (unless the tongues are interpreted).

"I wish you all spoke with tongues, but even more that you prophesied; for he who prophesies is greater than he who speaks with tongues, unless indeed he interprets, that the church may receive edification" (1 Corinthians 14:5).

Prophesying is for the believer.

"Therefore tongues are for a sign, not to those who believe but to unbelievers; but prophesying is not for unbelievers but for those who believe" (1 Corinthians 14:22).

NINE

Manifestation of Tongues Is Highly Desired in Private Prayer, but Should Be Limited in Church

In the fourteenth chapter of 1 Corinthians, Paul is careful to separate the usage of tongues in the church from their use in private prayer.

Jesus said that believers will speak in new tongues.
    "And these signs will follow those who be-lieve: In My name they will cast out demons; they will speak with new tongues" (Mark 16:17).

When you pray in a tongue that is unknown to you, you pray directly to God in the Spirit.

"For he who speaks in a tongue does not speak to men but to God, for no one understands him"(1 Corinthians 14:2).

You pray to God in spiritual "mysteries."

"For he who speaks in a tongue does not speak to men but to God, for no one understands him; however, in the spirit he speaks mysteries" (1 Corinthians 14:2).

You worship God in spirit and in truth, as Jesus commanded.

"But the hour is coming, and now is, when the true worshipers will worship the Father in spirit and truth; for the Father is seeking such to worship Him. God is Spirit, and those who worship Him must worship in spirit and truth" (John 4:23–24).

"O Lord, open my lips, and my mouth shall show forth Your praise" (Psalm 51:15).

You edify yourself spiritually.

"He who speaks in a tongue edifies himself" (1 Corinthians 14:4).

"That He would grant you, according to the riches of His glory, to be strengthened with might through His Spirit in the inner man"

(Ephesians 3:16).

"The Spirit Himself bears witness with our spirit that we are children of God" (Romans 8:16).

"But you, beloved, [build] yourselves up on your most holy faith, praying in the Holy Spirit" (Jude 20).

You thank God with an absolute unselfish prayer, a perfect prayer.

"For you indeed give thanks well" (1 Corinthians 14:17).

You can know the meaning of, *"Pray without ceasing"* (1 Thessalonians 5:17).

When you do not know what to pray for, or are not sure how God wants you to pray about a situation, then pray in the Spirit, and you cannot miss.

"Likewise the Spirit also helps in our weaknesses. For we do not know what we should pray for as we ought" (Romans 8:26).

The Spirit will pray for your infirmities (and those of others) for you.

"But the Spirit Himself makes intercession for us with groanings which cannot be uttered. Now He who searches the hearts knows what

the mind of the Spirit is, because He makes intercession for the saints according to the will of God" (Romans 8:26–27).

Always pray in the Spirit, so that you are able to boldly proclaim the Gospel.

"Praying always with all prayer and supplication in the Spirit, being watchful to this end with all perseverance and supplication for all the saints; and for me, that utterance may be given to me, that I may open my mouth boldly to make known the mystery of the gospel, for which I am an ambassador in chains; that in it I may speak boldly, as I ought to speak" (Ephesians 6:18–20).

"But you shall receive power when the Holy Spirit has come upon you; and you shall be witnesses to Me in Jerusalem, and in all Judea and Samaria, and to the end of the earth" (Acts 1:8).

It is desirable that all believers speak in tongues.

"I wish you all spoke with tongues" (1 Corinthians 14:5).

"If anyone thinks himself to be a prophet or spiritual, let him acknowledge that the things which I write to you are the commandments of the Lord" (1 Corinthians 14:37).

The Lord commands that we do not forbid fellow believers to speak in tongues.

"Therefore, brethren, desire earnestly to prophesy, and do not forbid to speak with tongues" (1 Corinthians 14:39).

Praying in tongues is a glory.

"I thank my God I speak with tongues more than you all" (1 Corinthians 14:18).

Singing with the Spirit is also a glory and a joy.

"I will sing with the spirit, and I will also sing with the understanding." (1 Corinthians 14:15).

Remember the power of what you speak.

"Death and life are in the power of the tongue" (Proverbs 18:21).

TEN

Manifestation of Tongues in the Church

All manifestations of the Spirit are to *"be done decently and in order"* (1 Corinthians 14:40).

In the church, praying in tongues should always be followed by interpretation.

"He who prophesies is greater than he who speaks with tongues, unless indeed he interprets, that the church may receive edification" (1 Corinthians 14:5).

Pray for interpretation.

"Therefore let him who speaks in a tongue pray that he may interpret" (1 Corinthians 14:13).

"If anyone speaks in a tongue, let there be two or at the most three, each in turn, and let one interpret" (1 Corinthians 14:27).

If there is no interpreter, then keep silent, but pray in tongues under your breath if you so desire.

"But if there is no interpreter, let him keep silent in church, and let him speak to himself and to God" (1 Corinthians 14:28).

Tongues and interpretation are to be of a limited number.

"Therefore if the whole church comes together in one place, and all speak with tongues, and there come in those who are uninformed or unbelievers, will they not say that you are out of your mind?" (1 Corinthians 14:23).

"If anyone speaks in a tongue, let there be two or at the most three, each in turn, and let one interpret" (1 Corinthians 14:27).

Remember, praying in tongues is a commandment of the Lord and is not to be forbidden.

"The things which I write to you are the commandments of the Lord" (1 Corinthians 14:37).

"Therefore, brethren, desire earnestly to

prophesy, and do not forbid to speak with tongues" (1 Corinthians 14:39).

Also remember that the Lord's church is even where only two or three are gathered together in His name. Thus, a prayer group is His church.

"For where two or three are gathered together in My name, I am there in the midst of them" (Matthew 18:20).

ELEVEN

What Should We Do with the Power Given to Us by the Baptism in the Holy Spirit?

Jesus' effective ministry commenced after this baptism. We ought to follow His example.

"Then Jesus came from Galilee to John at the Jordan to be baptized by him. And John tried to prevent Him, saying, 'I need to be baptized by You, and are You coming to me?' But Jesus answered and said to him, 'Permit it to be so now, for thus it is fitting for us to fulfill all righteousness.' Then he allowed Him. When He had been baptized, Jesus came up immediately from the water; and behold, the heavens

were opened to Him, and He saw the Spirit of God descending like a dove and alighting upon Him. And suddenly a voice came from heaven, saying, 'This is My beloved Son, in whom I am well pleased'" (Matthew 3:13–17).

"It came to pass in those days that Jesus came from Nazareth of Galilee, and was baptized by John in the Jordan. And immediately, coming up from the water, He saw the heavens parting and the Spirit descending upon Him like a dove. Then a voice came from heaven, 'You are My beloved Son, in whom I am well pleased'" (Mark 1:9–11).

"When all the people were baptized, it came to pass that Jesus also was baptized; and while He prayed, the heaven was opened. And the Holy Spirit descended in bodily form like a dove upon Him, and a voice came from heaven which said, 'You are My beloved Son; in You I am well pleased'" (Luke 3:21–22).

"The next day John saw Jesus coming toward him, and said, 'Behold! The Lamb of God who takes away the sin of the world! This is He of whom I said, "After me comes a Man who is preferred before me, for He was before me." I did not know Him; but that He should be revealed to Israel, therefore I came baptizing with water.' And John bore witness, saying, 'I saw the Spirit descending from heaven like a dove,

and He remained upon Him. I did not know Him, but He who sent me to baptize with water said to me, "Upon whom you see the Spirit descending, and remaining on Him, this is He who baptizes with the Holy Spirit." And I have seen and testified that this is the Son of God" (John 1:29–34).

The effective ministry of the apostles and the other disciples, after the Resurrection, commenced after this baptism.

"But Peter, standing up with the eleven, raised his voice and said to them, 'Men of Judea and all who dwell in Jerusalem, let this be known to you, and heed my words. For these are not drunk, as you suppose, since it is only the third hour of the day. But this is what was spoken by the prophet Joel: "And it shall come to pass in the last days, says God, that I will pour out of My Spirit on all flesh; your sons and your daughters shall prophesy, your young men shall see visions, your old men shall dream dreams. And on My menservants and on My maidservants I will pour out My Spirit in those days; and they shall prophesy. I will show wonders in heaven above and signs in the earth beneath: blood and fire and vapor of smoke. The sun shall be turned into darkness, and the moon into blood, before the coming of the great

and awesome day of the LORD. And it shall
come to pass that whoever calls on the name of
the LORD shall be saved.'"...Then Peter said to
them, 'Repent, and let every one of you be baptized in the name of Jesus Christ for the remission of sins; and you shall receive the gift of the
Holy Spirit. For the promise is to you and to
your children, and to all who are afar off, as
many as the Lord our God will call.' And with
many other words he testified and exhorted
them, saying, 'Be saved from this perverse generation.' Then those who gladly received his
word were baptized; and that day about three
thousand souls were added to them" (Acts
2:14–21, 38–41).

Paul's ministry also began after this baptism.

"And Ananias went his way and entered
the house; and laying his hands on him he
said, 'Brother Saul, the Lord Jesus, who ap-
peared to you on the road as you came, has sent
me that you may receive your sight and be filled
with the Holy Spirit.' Immediately there fell
from his eyes something like scales, and he received his sight at once; and he arose and was
baptized" (Acts 9:17–18).

Get to know your Bible, read it, study it.

"It is the Spirit who gives life; the flesh

profits nothing. The words that I speak to you are spirit, and they are life" (John 6:63).

"But the Helper, the Holy Spirit, whom the Father will send in My name, He will teach you all things, and bring to your remembrance all things that I said to you" (John 14:26).

"But when the Helper comes, whom I shall send to you from the Father, the Spirit of truth who proceeds from the Father, He will testify of Me" (John 15:26).

"However, when He, the Spirit of truth, has come, He will guide you into all truth; for He will not speak on His own authority, but whatever He hears He will speak; and He will tell you things to come. He will glorify Me, for He will take of what is Mine and declare it to you. All things that the Father has are Mine. Therefore I said that He will take of Mine and declare it to you" (John 16:13–15).

Edify, strengthen, and build up yourself in spiritual growth, so as to be able to carry out the other commands of the Lord in His church.

"He who speaks in a tongue edifies himself" (1 Corinthians 14:4).

"That He would grant you, according to the riches of His glory, to be strengthened with might through His Spirit in the inner man" (Ephesians 3:16).

"But you, beloved, [build] yourselves up on your most holy faith, praying in the Holy Spirit" (Jude 20).

Edify, strengthen, and build up the church; be eager to excel in the manifestations of the Spirit in order to edify the church.

"Even so you, since you are zealous for spiritual gifts, let it be for the edification of the church that you seek to excel" (1 Corinthians 14:12).

"Yet in the church I would rather speak five words with my understanding, that I may teach others also, than ten thousand words in a tongue" (1 Corinthians 14:19).

"Whenever you come together, each of you has a psalm, has a teaching, has a tongue, has a revelation, has an interpretation. Let all things be done for edification" (1 Corinthians 14:26).

"For you can all prophesy one by one, that all may learn and all may be encouraged" (1 Corinthians 14:31).

"He who prophesies edifies the church. I wish you all spoke with tongues, but even more that you prophesied; for he who prophesies is greater than he who speaks with tongues, unless indeed he interprets, that the church may receive edification" (1 Corinthians 14:4–5).

"Therefore take heed to yourselves and to all the flock, among which the Holy Spirit has made you overseers, to shepherd the church of God which He purchased with His own blood" (Acts 20:28).

Be witnesses for Jesus Christ and the Gospel.

"Go therefore and make disciples of all the nations, baptizing them in the name of the Father and of the Son and of the Holy Spirit, teaching them to observe all things that I have commanded you; and lo, I am with you always, even to the end of the age" (Matthew 28:19–20).

"But if I cast out demons by the Spirit of God, surely the kingdom of God has come upon you" (Matthew 12:28).

"And He said to them, 'Go into all the world and preach the gospel to every creature. He who believes and is baptized will be saved; but he who does not believe will be condemned. And these signs will follow those who believe: In My name they will cast out demons; they will speak with new tongues; they will take up serpents; and if they drink anything deadly, it will by no means hurt them; they will lay hands on the sick, and they will recover.' So then, after the Lord had spoken to them, He was received up into heaven, and sat down at the right hand of God. And they went out and preached everywhere, the Lord

working with them and confirming the word through the accompanying signs" (Mark 16:15–20).

"Praying always with all prayer and supplication in the Spirit, being watchful to this end with all perseverance and supplication for all the saints; and for me, that utterance may be given to me, that I may open my mouth boldly to make known the mystery of the gospel, for which I am an ambassador in chains; that in it I may speak boldly, as I ought to speak" (Ephesians 6:18–20).

"That each of you should know how to possess his own vessel in sanctification and honor" (1 Thessalonians 4:4).

"And that repentance and remission of sins should be preached in His name to all nations, beginning at Jerusalem. And you are witnesses of these things. Behold, I send the Promise of My Father upon you; but tarry in the city of Jerusalem until you are endued with power from on high" (Luke 24:47–49).

"So Jesus said to them again, 'Peace to you! As the Father has sent Me, I also send you'" (John 20:21).

"But you shall receive power when the Holy Spirit has come upon you; and you shall be witnesses to Me in Jerusalem, and in all Judea and Samaria, and to the end of the earth" (Acts 1:8).

"Therefore take heed to yourselves and to all the flock, among which the Holy Spirit has made you overseers, to shepherd the church of God which He purchased with His own blood" (Acts 20:28).

Your body is now the temple of the Holy Spirit.

"Do you not know that you are the temple of God and that the Spirit of God dwells in you? If anyone defiles the temple of God, God will destroy him. For the temple of God is holy, which temple you are" (1 Corinthians 3:16–17).

"Or do you not know that your body is the temple of the Holy Spirit who is in you, whom you have from God, and you are not your own? For you were bought at a price; therefore glorify God in your body and in your spirit, which are God's" (1 Corinthians 6:19–20).

Walk in the Spirit.

"If we live in the Spirit, let us also walk in the Spirit. Let us not become conceited, provoking one another, envying one another" (Galatians 5:25–26).

Do not grieve the Holy Spirit.

"And do not grieve the Holy Spirit of God, by whom you were sealed for the day of redemption" (Ephesians 4:30).

TWELVE

What Is the Fruit
of the Holy Spirit?

The love of God in your heart.

"*Now hope does not disappoint, because the love of God has been poured out in our hearts by the Holy Spirit who was given to us*" (Romans 5:5).

Love for others.

"*Love suffers long and is kind; love does not envy; love does not parade itself, is not puffed up; does not behave rudely, does not seek its own, is not provoked, thinks no evil; does not rejoice in iniquity, but rejoices in the truth; bears all things, believes all things, hopes all things, endures all things. Love never fails*" (1

Corinthians 13:4–8).

"*And now abide faith, hope, love, these three; but the greatest of these is love*" (1 Corinthians 13:13).

The components of love: joy, peace, long-suffering, gentleness, goodness, faith, meekness, righteousness, temperance, truth, power, and a sound mind.

"*But the fruit of the Spirit is love, joy, peace, longsuffering, kindness, goodness, faithfulness, gentleness, self-control. Against such there is no law*" (Galatians 5:22–23).

"*For the kingdom of God is not eating and drinking, but righteousness and peace and joy in the Holy Spirit*" (Romans 14:17).

"*For the fruit of the Spirit is in all goodness, righteousness, and truth*" (Ephesians 5:9).

"*For God has not given us a spirit of fear, but of power and of love and of a sound mind*" (2 Timothy 1:7).

"'*He who believes in Me, as the Scripture has said, out of his heart will flow rivers of living water.*' *But this He spoke concerning the Spirit, whom those believing in Him would receive; for the Holy Spirit was not yet given, because Jesus was not yet glorified*" (John 7:38–39).

Remember, you are no holier after receiving the baptism than you were before. But you now potentially have the power of Jesus within you to overcome evil. The Lord God lets it be your choice, your free will, as to how you will use this wonderful gift of God, or whether you will bury this talent (Matthew 25:14–30) in the earth.

THIRTEEN

How to Receive the Baptism in the Holy Spirit

Become converted, and then become as a little child.

"*Assuredly, I say to you, unless you are converted and become as little children, you will by no means enter the kingdom of heaven*" (Matthew 18:3).

"*Assuredly, I say to you, whoever does not receive the kingdom of God as a little child will by no means enter it*" (Mark 10:15).

Conversion must come first.

"*I will give you a new heart and put a new spirit within you; I will take the heart of stone out of your flesh and give you a heart of flesh. I will put My Spirit within you and cause you to walk in My statutes, and you will keep My judgments and do them"* (Ezekiel 36:26–27).

"Most assuredly, I say to you, unless one is born again, he cannot see the kingdom of God" (John 3:3).

"Most assuredly, I say to you, unless one is born of water and the Spirit, he cannot enter the kingdom of God" (John 3:5).

"Then Peter said to them, 'Repent, and let every one of you be baptized in the name of Jesus Christ for the remission of sins; and you shall receive the gift of the Holy Spirit. For the promise is to you and to your children, and to all who are afar off, as many as the Lord our God will call'" (Acts 2:38–39).

"Now when the apostles who were at Jerusalem heard that Samaria had received the word of God, they sent Peter and John to them, who, when they had come down, prayed for them that they might receive the Holy Spirit. For as yet He had fallen upon none of them. They had only been baptized in the name of the Lord Jesus. Then they laid hands on them, and they received the Holy Spirit" (Acts 8:14–17).

Obey the Great Commandment.

"Then one of them, a lawyer, asked Him a question, testing Him, and saying, 'Teacher,

*which is the great commandment in the law?'
Jesus said to him, '"You shall love the LORD
your God with all your heart, with all your
soul, and with all your mind." This is the first
and great commandment'"* (Matthew 22:35–
38).

*"So he answered and said, '"You shall love
the LORD your God with all your heart, with all
your soul, with all your strength, and with all
your mind," and "your neighbor as yourself"'"*
(Luke 10:27).

Obey God.

*"And we are His witnesses to these things,
and so also is the Holy Spirit whom God has
given to those who obey Him"* (Acts 5:32).

Have faith.

*"When the Day of Pentecost had fully come,
they were all with one accord in one place. And
suddenly there came a sound from heaven, as of
a rushing mighty wind, and it filled the whole
house where they were sitting. Then there ap-
peared to them divided tongues, as of fire, and
one sat upon each of them. And they were all
filled with the Holy Spirit and began to speak
with other tongues, as the Spirit gave them utterance"* (Acts 2:1–4).

"And when they had prayed, the place

*where they were assembled together was
shaken; and they were all filled with the Holy
Spirit, and they spoke the word of God with
boldness"* (Acts 4:31).

*"While Peter was still speaking these
words, the Holy Spirit fell upon all those who
heard the word"* (Acts 10:44).

**Let your faith stand in the power of God, not
in the wisdom of men.**

*"And my speech and my preaching were
not with persuasive words of human wisdom,
but in demonstration of the Spirit and of power,
that your faith should not be in the wisdom of
men but in the power of God. However, we
speak wisdom among those who are mature, yet
not the wisdom of this age, nor of the rulers of
this age, who are coming to nothing. But we
speak the wisdom of God in a mystery, the hidden wisdom which God ordained before the
ages for our glory, which none of the rulers of
this age knew; for had they known, they would
not have crucified the Lord of glory"* (1 Corinthians 2:4–8).

Determine to know only Christ crucified.

*"For I determined not to know anything
among you except Jesus Christ and Him crucified"* (1 Corinthians 2:2).

Relax and surrender every bit of yourself to God, especially your mind and your pride in intellect and worldly wisdom, for they mean nothing to God and are foolishness to Him.

"For Christ did not send me to baptize, but to preach the gospel, not with wisdom of words, lest the cross of Christ should be made of no effect. For the message of the cross is foolishness to those who are perishing, but to us who are being saved it is the power of God. For it is written: 'I will destroy the wisdom of the wise, and bring to nothing the understanding of the prudent'" (1 Corinthians 1:17–19).

"Inasmuch as these people draw near with their mouths and honor Me with their lips, but have removed their hearts far from Me, and their fear toward Me is taught by the commandment of men, therefore, behold, I will again do a marvelous work among this people, a marvelous work and a wonder; for the wisdom of their wise men shall perish, and the understanding of their prudent men shall be hidden" (Isaiah 29:13–14).

"Let no one deceive himself. If anyone among you seems to be wise in this age, let him become a fool that he may become wise. For the wisdom of this world is foolishness with God. For it is written, 'He catches the wise in their own craftiness'" (1 Corinthians 3:18–19).

"But He gives more grace. Therefore He says: 'God resists the proud, but gives grace to the humble.' Therefore submit to God. Resist the devil and he will flee from you" (James 4:6–7).

"Humble yourselves in the sight of the Lord, and He will lift you up" (James 4:10).

Your education can be a hindrance. D.D.'s and Ph.D.'s have a rough time receiving the Spirit until they set aside their human wisdom.

"Where is the wise? Where is the scribe? Where is the disputer of this age? Has not God made foolish the wisdom of this world? For since, in the wisdom of God, the world through wisdom did not know God, it pleased God through the foolishness of the message preached to save those who believe. For Jews request a sign, and Greeks seek after wisdom; but we preach Christ crucified, to the Jews a stumbling block and to the Greeks foolishness, but to those who are called, both Jews and Greeks, Christ the power of God and the wisdom of God. Because the foolishness of God is wiser than men, and the weakness of God is stronger than men. For you see your calling, brethren, that not many wise according to the flesh, not many mighty, not many noble, are called. But God has chosen the foolish things of

the world to put to shame the wise, and God has chosen the weak things of the world to put to shame the things which are mighty; and the base things of the world and the things which are despised God has chosen, and the things which are not, to bring to nothing the things that are" (1 Corinthians 1:20–28).

"Let no one deceive himself. If anyone among you seems to be wise in this age, let him become a fool that he may become wise. For the wisdom of this world is foolishness with God. For it is written, 'He catches the wise in their own craftiness'" (1 Corinthians 3:18–19).

The laying on of hands sometimes helps but is not always necessary.

"Then they laid hands on them, and they received the Holy Spirit" (Acts 8:17).

"While Peter was still speaking these words, the Holy Spirit fell upon all those who heard the word" (Acts 10:44).

"And when Paul had laid hands on them, the Holy Spirit came upon them, and they spoke with tongues and prophesied" (Acts 19:6).

"Therefore I remind you to stir up the gift of God which is in you through the laying on of my hands" (2 Timothy 1:6).

Ask the Father, and He will give you the baptism in the Holy Spirit.

"If a son asks for bread from any father among you, will he give him a stone? Or if he asks for a fish, will he give him a serpent instead of a fish? Or if he asks for an egg, will he offer him a scorpion? If you then, being evil, know how to give good gifts to your children, how much more will your heavenly Father give the Holy Spirit to those who ask Him!" (Luke 11:11–13).

Now, speak forth or sing with sounds that are entirely strange to you. Make the sounds (which are words in a language you do not know) by moving your tongue and lips. The sounds that come forth are a language of the Holy Spirit, praising and magnifying God in a perfect prayer.

"And they were all filled with the Holy Spirit and began to speak with other tongues, as the Spirit gave them utterance" (Acts 2:4).

"How is it that we hear, each in our own language in which we were born? Parthians and Medes and Elamites, those dwelling in Mesopotamia, Judea and Cappadocia, Pontus and Asia, Phrygia and Pamphylia, Egypt and the parts of Libya adjoining Cyrene, visitors from Rome, both Jews and proselytes, Cretans and Arabs; we

hear them speaking in our own tongues the wonderful works of God" (Acts 2:8–11).

"For they heard them speak with tongues and magnify God" (Acts 10:46).

Paul said that he desired to both pray and sing with the Spirit.

"What is the conclusion then? I will pray with the spirit, and I will also pray with the understanding. I will sing with the spirit, and I will also sing with the understanding" (1 Corinthians 14:15).

The sounds may come haltingly, or seem to stumble, at first, but this is entirely due to your own hesitancy and not that of the Spirit. He wants to praise God through your lips! So keep at it. Do not fail to pray with the Spirit several times, or more, each day. The wonder and glory of it will grow on you, and you will never be at a loss as to how to pray or what to pray about.

"Likewise the Spirit also helps in our weaknesses. For we do not know what we should pray for as we ought, but the Spirit Himself makes intercession for us with groanings which cannot be uttered. Now He who searches the hearts knows what the mind of the Spirit is, because He makes intercession for the saints according to the will of God" (Romans 8:26–27).

FOURTEEN

What May Happen After Receiving the Baptism in the Holy Spirit?

You may be tempted by Satan, as Jesus was (Matthew 4:1; Mark 1:12–13; Luke 4:1–2), to doubt that you have received the baptism. The Devil may cause you to think, "This is me doing the tongues; this is all foolishness." Here is the first test of your faith, for Satan is really interested in you now. Just continue praying in the Spirit, no matter how foolish it may sound, and Jesus will win out for you. For you now have His Spirit in you, the power of the Holy Spirit, to help you overcome Satan. Remember, "It is written" (Matthew 4:3–11; Luke 4:3–12).

You may be delivered up before persecutors.

"Behold, I send you out as sheep in the midst of wolves. Therefore be wise as serpents and harmless as doves. But beware of men, for they will deliver you up to councils and scourge you in their synagogues. You will be brought before governors and kings for My sake, as a testimony to them and to the Gentiles. But when they deliver you up, do not worry about how or what you should speak. For it will be given to you in that hour what you should speak; for it is not you who speak, but the Spirit of your Father who speaks in you. Now brother will deliver up brother to death, and a father his child; and children will rise up against parents and cause them to be put to death. And you will be hated by all for My name's sake. But he who endures to the end will be saved" (Matthew 10:16–22).

"But when they arrest you and deliver you up, do not worry beforehand, or premeditate what you will speak. But whatever is given you in that hour, speak that; for it is not you who speak, but the Holy Spirit" (Mark 13:11).

"Now when they bring you to the synagogues and magistrates and authorities, do not worry about how or what you should answer, or what you should say. For the Holy Spirit will teach you in that very hour what you ought to

say" (Luke 12:11–12).

"*But before all these things, they will lay their hands on you and persecute you, delivering you up to the synagogues and prisons. You will be brought before kings and rulers for My name's sake. But it will turn out for you as an occasion for testimony. Therefore settle it in your hearts not to meditate beforehand on what you will answer; for I will give you a mouth and wisdom which all your adversaries will not be able to contradict or resist*" (Luke 21:12–15).

"*Yes, and all who desire to live godly in Christ Jesus will suffer persecution*" (2 Timothy 3:12).

"*Beloved, do not think it strange concerning the fiery trial which is to try you, as though some strange thing happened to you; but rejoice to the extent that you partake of Christ's sufferings, that when His glory is revealed, you may also be glad with exceeding joy. If you are reproached for the name of Christ, blessed are you, for the Spirit of glory and of God rests upon you. On their part He is blasphemed, but on your part He is glorified*" (1 Peter 4:12–14).

You may be teaching and preaching.

"*Go therefore and make disciples of all the nations, baptizing them in the name of the Father and of the Son and of the Holy Spirit, teaching them to observe all things that I have commanded you; and lo, I am with you always, even to the end of the age"* (Matthew 28:19–20).

"And He said to them, 'Go into all the world and preach the gospel to every creature'" (Mark 16:15).

"And that repentance and remission of sins should be preached in His name to all nations, beginning at Jerusalem" (Luke 24:47).

"Praying always with all prayer and supplication in the Spirit, being watchful to this end with all perseverance and supplication for all the saints; and for me, that utterance may be given to me, that I may open my mouth boldly to make known the mystery of the gospel, for which I am an ambassador in chains; that in it I may speak boldly, as I ought to speak" (Ephesians 6:18–20).

You may be here for the coming of Christ for His church, when manifestations of the Holy Spirit will cease, for they will no longer be needed in His presence.

"But whether there are prophecies, they will fail; whether there are tongues, they will cease; whether there is knowledge, it will vanish away. For we know in part and we prophesy in part. But when that which is perfect has come, then that which is in part will be done

away" (1 Corinthians 13:8–10).

You may be tempted to use tongues only occasionally in private prayer. Don't stunt your spiritual growth; rather, always pray in the Spirit.

"Praying always with all prayer and supplication in the Spirit, being watchful to this end with all perseverance and supplication for all the saints" (Ephesians 6:18).

"I thank my God I speak with tongues more than you all" (1 Corinthians 14:18).

"Do not neglect the gift that is in you" (1 Timothy 4:14).

FIFTEEN

The Unforgivable Sin: Blasphemy against the Holy Spirit

All sins and blasphemies will be forgiven except that against the Holy Spirit.

"Therefore I say to you, every sin and blasphemy will be forgiven men, but the blasphemy against the Spirit will not be forgiven men. Anyone who speaks a word against the Son of Man, it will be forgiven him; but whoever speaks against the Holy Spirit, it will not be forgiven him, either in this age or in the age to come" (Matthew 12:31–32).

"Assuredly, I say to you, all sins will be forgiven the sons of men, and whatever blasphemies they may utter; but he who blasphemes

against the Holy Spirit never has forgiveness, but is subject to eternal condemnation" (Mark 3:28–29).

"And anyone who speaks a word against the Son of Man, it will be forgiven him; but to him who blasphemes against the Holy Spirit, it will not be forgiven" (Luke 12:10).

"For it is impossible for those who were once enlightened, and have tasted the heavenly gift, and have become partakers of the Holy Spirit, and have tasted the good word of God and the powers of the age to come, if they fall away, to renew them again to repentance, since they crucify again for themselves the Son of God, and put Him to an open shame" (Hebrews 6:4–6).

SIXTEEN

Reasons Used to Reject the Baptism in the Holy Spirit

Rejection of the Holy Spirit took place even before Christ, when the Holy Spirit was with the prophets.

"You stiffnecked and uncircumcised in heart and ears! You always resist the Holy Spirit; as your fathers did, so do you" (Acts 7:51).

Full acceptance of God, Jesus, and the Holy Spirit requires the faith of a child.

"Assuredly, I say to you, unless you are converted and become as little children, you

will by no means enter the kingdom of heaven" (Matthew 18:3).

"Assuredly, I say to you, whoever does not receive the kingdom of God as a little child will by no means enter it" (Mark 10:15).

Jesus was rejected by those in high places, by most of the religious leaders, by the successful businesspeople, by the intellectuals, and even by some of His disciples who "fell away" from Him. So it is today with the baptism in the Holy Spirit.

"From that time many of His disciples went back and walked with Him no more" (John 6:66).

"Nevertheless even among the rulers many believed in Him, but because of the Pharisees they did not confess Him, lest they should be put out of the synagogue; for they loved the praise of men more than the praise of God" (John 12:42–43).

"You stiffnecked and uncircumcised in heart and ears! You always resist the Holy Spirit; as your fathers did, so do you" (Acts 7:51).

"For you see your calling, brethren, that not many wise according to the flesh, not many mighty, not many noble, are called" (1 Corinthians 1:26).

Prior to their baptism in the Holy Spirit, hundreds of clergymen and laypeople of the so-called denominational churches believed in one or more of the objections set forth below. But when they followed Jesus' command to search the Scriptures, their objections were melted away in the purifying fires of God's Holy Word.

"You search the Scriptures, for in them you think you have eternal life; and these are they which testify of Me" (John 5:39).

"And my speech and my preaching were not with persuasive words of human wisdom, but in demonstration of the Spirit and of power, that your faith should not be in the wisdom of men but in the power of God. However, we speak wisdom among those who are mature, yet not the wisdom of this age, nor of the rulers of this age, who are coming to nothing. But we speak the wisdom of God in a mystery, the hidden wisdom which God ordained before the ages for our glory, which none of the rulers of this age knew; for had they known, they would not have crucified the Lord of glory" (1 Corinthians 2:4–8).

Some principal objections to the baptism are as follows.

Objection #1
The baptism in the Holy Spirit was only for the early church.

a. This is an attempt to limit God. There are no man-made time limitations in God's kingdom.

"But, beloved, do not forget this one thing, that with the Lord one day is as a thousand years, and a thousand years as one day" (2 Peter 3:8).

"But this is what was spoken by the prophet Joel: 'And it shall come to pass in the last days, says God, that I will pour out of My Spirit on all flesh; your sons and your daughters shall prophesy, your young men shall see visions, your old men shall dream dreams. And on My menservants and on My maidservants I will pour out My Spirit in those days; and they shall prophesy. I will show wonders in heaven above and signs in the earth beneath: blood and fire and vapor of smoke. The sun shall be turned into darkness, and the moon into blood, before the coming of the great and awesome day of the LORD. And it shall come to pass that whoever calls on the name of the LORD shall be saved'" (Acts 2:16–21).

"God, who at various times and in various ways spoke in time past to the fathers by the prophets, has in these last days spoken to us by

His Son, whom He has appointed heir of all things, through whom also He made the worlds" (Hebrews 1:1–2).

"[We] are kept by the power of God through faith for salvation ready to be revealed in the last time" (1 Peter 1:5).

"He indeed was foreordained before the foundation of the world, but was manifest in these last times for you" (1 Peter 1:20).

b. The Lord can do anything and everything today that He has ever done—as He will, where He will, when He will, and with whom He will.

"Jesus Christ is the same yesterday, today, and forever" (Hebrews 13:8).

c. God does not have His children waste His time by having them read something in His Word that is of no use to them today.

"Most assuredly, I say to you, he who believes in Me, the works that I do he will do also; and greater works than these he will do, because I go to My Father" (John 14:12).

d. With the baptism now being received by both the clergy and laity of most Christian churches, this is a further fulfillment of the prophecy of Joel that began at Pentecost.

"And it shall come to pass afterward that I will pour out My Spirit on all flesh" (Joel 2:28).

"For the promise is to you and to your children, and to all who are afar off, as many as the Lord our God will call" (Acts 2:39).

"That the Gentiles should be fellow heirs, of the same body, and partakers of His promise in Christ through the gospel" (Ephesians 3:6).

Objection #2
Tongues are of the Devil.

a. This statement is not supported either by the Scriptures or by experience. If the statement were true, the Devil, with his hatred of Jesus, would use tongues to have us curse our Lord. The Scriptures tell us not only that this is impossible, but also that Satan and his minions cannot understand tongues. Only the Holy Spirit has the gift of the true interpretation.

"Therefore I make known to you that no one speaking by the Spirit of God calls Jesus accursed, and no one can say that Jesus is Lord except by the Holy Spirit" (1 Corinthians 12:3).

"For he who speaks in a tongue does not speak to men but to God, for no one understands him; however, in the spirit he speaks mysteries" (1 Corinthians 14:2).

"But we speak the wisdom of God in a mystery, the hidden wisdom which God ordained before the ages for our glory, which none of the rulers of this age knew; for had they known, they would not have crucified the Lord of glory" (1 Corinthians 2:7–8).

b. Experience proves that this is a lie of Satan, because the Devil hates tongues. Often Satan attacks people who are calling upon the name of Jesus and His precious shed blood, who are giving the word of their testimony, and who are praying in tongues. Many times these people can actually feel Satan flee, and they feel the precious love of Christ take over while they are praying in tongues.

"And they overcame him by the blood of the Lamb and by the word of their testimony" (Revelation 12:11).

"I thank my God I speak with tongues more than you all" (1 Corinthians 14:18).

c. Experience shows that people who pray often in tongues in their private devotions achieve the following results:

- They love God more and more as the Father, as the Son, and as the Holy Spirit.
- They understand how a person can die

99

joyfully.
- They love their neighbor, particularly those whom they formerly considered "unlovable."
- They love the Bible above all other literature.
- They love to witness and talk about Jesus.
- They have a holy joy in the midst of pain and tribulation.

d. This is what the baptism in the Holy Spirit is accomplishing, through the gift of speaking in unknown tongues, in people of the old-line denominational churches who receive this baptism from God. How can tongues be of the Devil?

Objection #3
Tongues are the least of the gifts.

a. There is no direct scriptural reference to this effect, but note what Paul said about the gift of speaking in tongues.

"I thank my God I speak with tongues more than you all" (1 Corinthians 14:18).

"I wish you all spoke with tongues" (1 Corinthians 14:5).

"Do not forbid to speak with tongues" (1 Corinthians 14:39).

b. This attack may be answered with Jesus' own statements about "the least."

"If you then are not able to do the least, why are you anxious for the rest?" (Luke 12:26).

"Whoever therefore breaks one of the least of these commandments, and teaches men so, shall be called least in the kingdom of heaven; but whoever does and teaches them, he shall be called great in the kingdom of heaven" (Matthew 5:19).

"The kingdom of heaven is like a mustard seed, which a man took and sowed in his field, which indeed is the least of all the seeds; but when it is grown it is greater than the herbs and becomes a tree, so that the birds of the air come and nest in its branches" (Matthew 13:31–32).

"And the King will answer and say to them, 'Assuredly, I say to you, inasmuch as you did it to one of the least of these My brethren, you did it to Me'" (Matthew 25:40).

"Whoever receives this little child in My name receives Me; and whoever receives Me receives Him who sent Me. For he who is least among you all will be great" (Luke 9:48).

"He who is faithful in what is least is faithful also in much; and he who is unjust in what is least is unjust also in much" (Luke 16:10).

Objection #4
It is emotionalism.

a. **What did God give us emotions for? The Great Commandment is to love God with everything we have. How can you love, and leave out emotion? The soul or heart, one or the other, is the seat of the emotions, and we are commanded to love God with all our hearts and souls as well as our minds.**

"You shall love the LORD your God with all your heart, with all your soul, and with all your mind" (Matthew 22:37).

b. **What is music in our churches supposed to accomplish if it does not touch the emotions? If you see or hear about the antics of someone who has received the baptism, remember that if the love of God is in the heart, the antics are never undignified in His eyes, although they may be in the eyes of man.**

"But God hath chosen the foolish things of the world to confound the wise" (1 Corinthians 1:27 KJV).

"Jesus wept" (John 11:35).

"Who, in the days of His flesh, when He had offered up prayers and supplications, with vehement cries and tears to Him who was able to save Him from death, and was heard because

of His godly fear, though He was a Son, yet He learned obedience by the things which He suffered. And having been perfected, He became the author of eternal salvation to all who obey Him" (Hebrews 5:7–9).

"So they were all amazed and perplexed, saying to one another, 'Whatever could this mean?' Others mocking said, 'They are full of new wine.' But Peter, standing up with the eleven, raised his voice and said to them, 'Men of Judea and all who dwell in Jerusalem, let this be known to you, and heed my words. For these are not drunk, as you suppose, since it is only the third hour of the day. But this is what was spoken by the prophet Joel'" (Acts 2:12–16).

c. Lukewarmness is despised by Jesus.

"I know your works, that you are neither cold nor hot. I could wish you were cold or hot. So then, because you are lukewarm, and neither cold nor hot, I will vomit you out of My mouth" (Revelation 3:15–16).

Objection #5
Tongues are not necessary, so we should leave them out of the Christian experience.

a. This is attempting to tell Jesus Christ how

His Holy Spirit is to behave. This is a way of forbidding to speak in tongues, which goes against the commandment of the Lord.

"If anyone thinks himself to be a prophet or spiritual, let him acknowledge that the things which I write to you are the commandments of the Lord. But if anyone is ignorant, let him be ignorant. Therefore, brethren, desire earnestly to prophesy, and do not forbid to speak with tongues" (1 Corinthians 14:37–39).

b. This is also a failure to fully surrender everything to God, for the tongue is the member of the body that can do the most good and the most harm.

"We all stumble in many things. If anyone does not stumble in word, he is a perfect man, able also to bridle the whole body. Indeed, we put bits in horses' mouths that they may obey us, and we turn their whole body. Look also at ships: although they are so large and are driven by fierce winds, they are turned by a very small rudder wherever the pilot desires. Even so the tongue is a little member and boasts great things. See how great a forest a little fire kindles! And the tongue is a fire, a world of iniquity. The tongue is so set among our members that it defiles the whole body, and sets on fire the course of nature; and it is set on fire by hell.

For every kind of beast and bird, of reptile and creature of the sea, is tamed and has been tamed by mankind. But no man can tame the tongue. It is an unruly evil, full of deadly poison. With it we bless our God and Father, and with it we curse men, who have been made in the similitude of God. Out of the same mouth proceed blessing and cursing. My brethren, these things ought not to be so" (James 3:2–10).

Objection #6
These people are selfish; they think they have something that others do not have.

a. Of course they have, and so do those who have salvation! The Scripture tells us that those who have received Christ are a special people.

"[Christ] *gave Himself for us, that He might redeem us from every lawless deed and purify for Himself His own special people, zealous for good works"* (Titus 2:14).

"But you are a chosen generation, a royal priesthood, a holy nation, His own special people, that you may proclaim the praises of Him who called you out of darkness into His marvelous light" (1 Peter 2:9).

b. Almost everyone has something more in

some respect than others—more education, more money, better health, better looks, a better marriage, more freedom, or more love for God. But those with the full infilling of the Holy Spirit are far from selfish, for they all want everyone else to have it, too, and will lovingly spend all kinds of time and effort to help others to receive it.

"As each one has received a gift, minister it to one another, as good stewards of the manifold grace of God" (1 Peter 4:10).

Objection #7
Sure, tongues are scriptural, but I don't need them for assurance that I have the baptism.

a. The one manifestation that satisfied the apostles and the other disciples that a person had received the baptism, was speaking in an unknown tongue.

"Now the apostles and brethren who were in Judea heard that the Gentiles had also received the word of God. And when Peter came up to Jerusalem, those of the circumcision contended with him, saying, 'You went in to uncircumcised men and ate with them!' But Peter explained it to them in order from the beginning, saying:...'As I began to speak, the Holy Spirit fell

upon them, as upon us at the beginning....If therefore God gave them the same gift as He gave us when we believed on the Lord Jesus Christ, who was I that I could withstand God?' When they heard these things they became silent; and they glorified God, saying, 'Then God has also granted to the Gentiles repentance to life'" (Acts 11:1–4, 15, 17–18).

b. There are many people, especially clergy, who have felt this way until they have come in close contact with people who have fully received. Then, when the former finally received the fullness of the baptism, they felt that they had not had it before — that the Spirit had been with them but not in them.

"The Spirit of truth, whom the world cannot receive, because it neither sees Him nor knows Him; but you know Him, for He dwells with you and will be in you" (John 14:17).

c. Paul felt that praying in an unknown tongue went far beyond just an assurance of having received the baptism.

"I wish you all spoke with tongues" (1 Corinthians 14:5).

"I thank my God I speak with tongues more than you all" (1 Corinthians 14:18).

Objection #8
Why don't the Scriptures record that Jesus spoke in an unknown tongue?

a. How could He? What tongues were unknown to Jesus? He knew all languages.

"Then to Him was given dominion and glory and a kingdom, that all peoples, nations, and languages should serve Him" (Daniel 7:14).

"For He whom God has sent speaks the words of God, for God does not give the Spirit by measure" (John 3:34).

b. Jesus was never limited and never will be.

"Jesus Christ is the same yesterday, today, and forever" (Hebrews 13:8).

People who receive the baptism in the Holy Spirit must be hungry enough for Jesus to want to receive everything that He has for them. They must do so with such faith that they will gladly accept whatever comes in any way that He chooses to give it.

"Nevertheless not My will, but Yours, be done" (Luke 22:42).

SEVENTEEN

Is It True? Is It Real? Does It Work?

The documented and oral testimonies of thousands of clergymen and laypeople from practically every Christian church that has received this wonderful blessing, bear witness that the answer is a glorious "Yes!" They will tell you that the Bible has become truly alive to them.

"But the Helper, the Holy Spirit, whom the Father will send in My name, He will teach you all things, and bring to your remembrance all things that I said to you" (John 14:26).

The Christ who is now in these believers speaks words of wisdom and of knowledge, heals the sick, works miracles, strengthens

faith, discerns good and evil spirits, prays in and interprets tongues, and prophesies.

"But the manifestation of the Spirit is given to each one for the profit of all: for to one is given the word of wisdom through the Spirit, to another the word of knowledge through the same Spirit, to another faith by the same Spirit, to another gifts of healings by the same Spirit, to another the working of miracles, to another prophecy, to another discerning of spirits, to another different kinds of tongues, to another the interpretation of tongues" (1 Corinthians 12:7–10).

It is indeed the age of the Holy Spirit.

"And it shall come to pass afterward that I will pour out My Spirit on all flesh; your sons and your daughters shall prophesy, your old men shall dream dreams, your young men shall see visions. And also on My menservants and on My maidservants I will pour out My Spirit in those days" (Joel 2:28–29).

Keep one last thing in mind.

"But as it is written: 'Eye has not seen, nor ear heard, nor have entered into the heart of man the things which God has prepared for those who love Him.' But God has revealed

them to us through His Spirit. For the Spirit searches all things, yes, the deep things of God" (1 Corinthians 2:9–10).